Grand Prix

Sandra Woodcock

Published in association with The Basic Skills Agency

Hodder & Stoughton

A MEMBER OF THE HODDER HEADLINE

Acknowledgements

Cover: Sportsphoto Ltd

Illustrations: pp 2, 6, 14 Popperfoto; pp10, 17 EMPICS Ltd; p 20 Popperfoto/Reuters

Every effort has been made to trace copyright holders of material reproduced in this book. Any rights not acknowledged will be acknowledged in subsequent printings if notice is given to the publisher.

Orders; please contact Bookpoint Ltd, 39 Milton Park, Abingdon, Oxon OX14 4TD. Telephone: (44) 01235 400414, Fax: (44) 01235 400454. Lines are open from 9.00–6.00, Monday to Saturday, with a 24 hour message answering service.
Email address: orders@bookpoint.co.uk

British Library Cataloguing in Publication Data
A catalogue record for this title is available from the British Library

ISBN 0 340 74713 7

First published 2000
Impression number   10 9 8 7 6 5 4 3 2 1
Year   2005 2004 2003 2002 2001 2000

Copyright © 2000 Sandra Woodcock

Typeset by GreenGate Publishing Services, Tonbridge, Kent.
Printed in Great Britain for Hodder and Stoughton Educational, a division of Hodder Headline Plc, 338 Euston Road, London NW1 3BH, Redwood Books, Trowbridge, Wilts

Contents

Formula One is the world's
number one motor sport.
It's a fast, exciting sport.
The cars are the best in the world.
The drivers are the most skilled in the world.
Formula One has millions of fans
all over the world.
In this book you can find out more about it.

1 The Early Days

As soon as cars were invented,
drivers wanted to race them.
The first races were on roads
from city to city.
But there were too many accidents.
So special circuits were made.

Many early races took place in France.
In French, 'Grand Prix' means grand prize.
At first the name was used for many races.
But today 'Grand Prix' is the name
for top Formula One races.

Today most Grand Prix races
are on special circuits.
But the Monaco Grand Prix
is held on the streets of the town.

The race for the Monaco Grand Prix.

Motor racing was controlled by
the FIA in Paris.
In 1947 the FIA set up two classes
of motor racing:
Formula One and Formula Two.
Formula One was for the fastest cars.
Soon after this, there were plans
to hold a World Championship.

The first Formula One
World Championship race
was in 1950 at Silverstone in Britain.
There were six other races in that first season.
All were held in different countries.

Italian drivers and cars were way ahead.
The first World Champion was Farina.
He drove an Alfa Romeo.

2 The Drivers

Formula One drivers
have built up their skills over a long time.
Many of them started in kart racing.
They may race Formula Three
or Formula Two cars first.

There is more to racing than just speed.
There is a lot to think about:
the circuit, the weather,
the car, the other drivers
and the tactics they will use.
Drivers need to concentrate very hard
all the time.
There has to be good team work too.

Every Formula One driver
wants to be World Champion.
The best driver has to do well
in all the Grand Prix races of the season.
There can be up to 16 races.
The races are held in different countries.

In each race,
the first six drivers to finish win points.
There are 10 points for the first place,
then 6–4–3–2–1 for the other five drivers.
The drivers add up their points
during the season.

The driver with the most points
at the end of the season
is World Champion.
In 1996 Damon Hill from Britain
was World Champion with 97 points.
In 1997 Villeneuve from Canada won,
with 81 points.

Juan Fangio winning the German Grand Prix.

3   Great Names

Every sport has its great heroes.
There are many great names in Formula One.
Some say that Fangio was the best.
He was racing between 1950 and 1958.
He was World Champion five times.

His 1957 win in the German Grand Prix
is one of the great races
in the history of the sport.
After a pit stop which took too long,
Fangio was a whole minute behind the leaders.
But he drove so well, he closed the gap.
The crowd could not believe it:
he gained eight or nine seconds on every lap.
He won the race
three seconds ahead of the others.

Formula One was very different then.
There were only eight races.
Fangio's speed in that race was 88.78 mph.
Today, a Grand Prix winner
might average 120 mph
and can go up to 200 mph.
But many modern drivers
would agree that Fangio deserves
his place in Formula One history.

4 Jackie Stewart

Jackie Stewart is one of Britain's
great racing drivers.
He was World Champion three times
(1969, 1971, 1973).
His best drive was in
the German Grand Prix in 1968.
The circuit was the Nurburgring.
Drivers call it 'The Ring'.
It was one of the hardest to drive
at the best of times.

There had been very heavy rain.
The start was delayed for one hour.
There were rivers of water around the circuit.
It was foggy.
Jackie Stewart did not think it was safe to drive.
But he had to do it.

The wet track was very dangerous.
There was so much spray, that people watching
could not tell one driver from another.
Jackie needed all his skills.

Jackie Stewart

But after one lap he was leading
by nine seconds.
He went on to gain time on every lap.
The other drivers were no problem.
He had to battle with the weather, in a wet hell.
Jackie won the race by four whole minutes.
It was the drive of his life.

Jackie was racing at a time when there were
many fatal accidents in the sport.
In 1970 Jochen Rindt crashed his car
and was killed.
At the end of the season,
Rindt had the most points.
Formula One had a dead man
as World Champion.

Jackie was shocked by the number of drivers
who were killed.
It made him think about
the risks he was taking.

Then in 1973 his team mate
was killed in a practice race.
Jackie gave up driving,
but he still worked in the sport.

He worked hard to make Formula One
safer for drivers.
He complained about The Ring in Germany.
He said it was too dangerous for the drivers.
Another driver who agreed with him
was Niki Lauda.

5 Niki Lauda

Niki was World Champion in 1975.
He knew The Ring well.
He knew there had been many accidents there.
In 1976 he wanted the drivers
to boycott The Ring.
But the votes went against him.
He had to race there.
At the start of the race,
someone gave him a photo
of Jochen Rindt's grave.

In this race, Niki crashed his car.
It bounced back onto the track
and was hit by another car.
It burst into flames.

Other drivers rushed to help him.
He was dragged from the burning car.
He had terrible burns
to his face, his head and his hands.
He had smoke and petrol fumes in his lungs.
He was in great pain.
He was only just alive.
Many people thought he would die.

June 1975 Niki Lauda in a Ferrari at Monza, Italy.

But Niki did not die.
People said he would never race again.
But only six weeks later he came back
to the Grand Prix in Italy.
He had bad scars and his face was still painful.
But he wanted to hold on to his world title.

At the end of the season,
he was still three points ahead.
But in Japan, he pulled out of the race.
Heavy rain had made the track dangerous.
His rival, James Hunt, stayed in
and finished third.
He now had one point more than Niki.
So Hunt was the 1976 World Champion.

1976 was not Niki's year.
But he went on to win two more world titles.
When he retired from driving,
he kept his interest in the sport
and still worked in Formula One.
He became a friend and a team mate
to a young French driver called Alain Prost.

6 Two Great Rivals: Prost and Senna

Alain Prost was one of the best drivers
in the 1980s.
He has been World Champion four times.
He has won 51 Grand Prix races –
more than any other driver
in the history of Formula One.

Prost has a nickname, 'The Professor'.
This is because he is good at
thinking about tactics.
He said that winning races
is not just about speed
it is about not making any mistakes.
Prost's biggest rival was a driver from Brazil
called Ayrton Senna.
They both drove McLaren cars.

They were both great drivers
but they did not get on well.
In the end Prost left the McLaren team
to drive for Ferrari.

Prost, Senna and Damon Hill celebrating at the Australian
Grand Prix in November 1993.

1994 was a tragic year for Formula One.
In one weekend in Italy, there were two deaths.
In a practice race,
Ratzenberger crashed into a wall
at almost 200 mph,
and died from a broken neck.
The next day in the race, Ayrton Senna
lost control of his car and hit a wall at 135 mph.
Senna died in hospital.
There had not been a death
in a Formula One race for 12 years.
Now two drivers had been killed
on the same weekend.

7 Drivers in the 1990s

In the 1990s the two main rivals
were Damon Hill and Michael Schumacher.
There were keen contests and hot disputes
between the two of them.
1994 was the worst year.
After Senna's death, the two of them
were in a battle to win the title.

At the end of the season,
Schumacher won the World Championship,
but he had a lot of trouble on the way.
At Silverstone he broke the rules on starting
and was banned for two races.

Later in the season,
his team Benetton were in trouble.
One of their cars burst into flames in a pit stop.
There was a wall of fire
around the driver and the crew.
They were lucky that day – nobody died,
there were only burns.
But Benetton had to answer questions
about their safety.

Damon Hill (Williams) close behind Michael Schumacher (Benetton) in the early stages of the Australian Grand Prix.

Hill and Schumacher disliked each other.
By the time they got to
the last race of the season,
there was only one point between them.
The last race was in Australia.
Schumacher was ahead of Hill
but his car touched the side of a wall
and was damaged.
As Hill came around the comer,
Schumacher's car turned into him.
Now Hill's car was damaged as well.
Both drivers were out of the race.

Schumacher had won the Championship
by one point.
But there was a black cloud over him.
Many people said that he had stopped Hill
on purpose.
He was World Champion for the first time
but he was called a cheat.
1994 had been a terrible year for Formula One.
It was not a good way to end it.

In 1995 Schumacher won again.
This time by 33 points!
The next year Damon Hill won the title,
Jacques Villeneuve came second
and Schumacher was third.

In 1997 Schumacher was again in trouble
for crashing into Villeneuve in the last race.
Second place was taken away from him
because of that.
Villeneuve won the title.
As the l990s end,
the top drivers are Schumacher, Villeneuve
and Mika Hakkinen who won the 1998 title.

8 The Teams

Winning Formula One is a team effort.
The driver who wins is a star
but behind him is a massive team effort.
The crews in the pits
can change tyres and refuel in seconds.
Their skills can help the driver to win.

The cars have to be the best.
Formula One is always changing.
The top teams have to keep up with their rivals
and try to get ahead.
The Constructors Cup is for the best car
of the season. All the teams are keen to win it.

Ferrari are one of the best known teams
and have been in Formula One from the beginning.
Ferrari were the most successful team
in Formula One
but they have not won a World Championship
in the last 20 years.
The top teams they have to beat today
are McLaren and Williams.

When Frank Williams came into Formula One
in the 1970s, he found it very hard
and was always short of money.
Williams were the underdogs.
However, he was determined to make it,
and today Williams are a top team.

Bruce McLaren formed his own team in 1966.
He drove his own cars for a time.
In 1970 he died in a crash
while he was testing one of the cars.
But in the 1990s his team
are at the top of Formula One.

A driver may work for different teams
in his racing career.
The driver and the team
must work well together
to get the best out of the car.

9 Money and Sponsors

Formula One is said to be a sport of the rich.
It costs millions of pounds to run a team,
even for one season.
The costs include research,
building the car and testing.
The drivers have to be paid.
Then, there is the cost of the engine,
the tyres and the fuel.
There are many other costs.

Formula One has to have sponsors.
If an engine name is seen on a winning car
it's a very good advert for the firm.
The engine name is part of the team name.
The name Renault is linked with
the Williams team.
Honda was linked with McLaren
for many years.

Formula One is a very popular TV sport,
second only to football.
It is watched all over the world.
There are Formula One magazines,
videos, models and toys.
So many firms
want to get their names on the cars.
Tobacco firms have always been big sponsors.
But many people say that the sport
should not be linked to smoking.
Some banks are now Formula One sponsors.

Benetton make and sell clothes.
They set up their own Formula One team
to promote the name.
It's a winning team, so other firms
are keen to sponsor them.

The winning teams attract the money.
It is hard for new teams to get into the sport.

10 The Rules of Formula One

The Grand Prix races take three days.
The first two days are for practice on the track.
Drivers have to take part in a race to qualify
and to get their starting position.
The fastest driver in the qualifying race
gets the best starting position in the real race.
This is called the pole position.

In the race the driver must watch
for flag signals.
A yellow flag warns of danger
and bans overtaking.
A red flag means the race has been stopped.
A black flag with an orange spot
means the driver has a car problem
and must go into the pit.
If the black flag has
the driver's car number on it
then he must pull in for a penalty stop
or maybe a ban from the race.
The black and white checked flag
shows the end of the race.

There arc many rules about safety.
The FIA has to keep a close watch
on new car designs.

Car design changes so that cars can go faster.
The cars must not become death traps.

The less air there is under a car,
the faster it can corner.
So Formula One cars are very low,
almost on the ground.
There are strict rules about the size
and weight of the car.
Engines cannot be more than three litres.
They cannot have more than 12 cylinders.
There are rules about the tyres used
and how many changes can be made.

The driver must wear a six-point harness.
But he must be able to get out of the car
within seven seconds.
The car has to pass a number of crash tests
before it can enter a race.

Circuits have been made much safer too.
In modern Formula One racing,
cars crash at high speeds
but drivers can still walk away unhurt.

Formula One now has a very good safety record.
But fans still think it is
the most exciting sport in the world!